To Sarah, Aurora, and Isis

The real reason I keep drawing

INTRODUCTION

Ages ago, the British writer Somerset Maugham declared that "To eat well in England, you should eat breakfast three times a day." Until the end of the twentieth century, that was the beginning and end of smart dining advice about the country. However, in the past two decades or so, something marvelous happened. In 2012, none other than the esteemed French chef Joël Robuchon, who accrued more than thirty Michelin stars in his lifetime, made headlines for arguing that "London is very possibly the gastronomic capital of the world."

Robuchon was recognizing that a thriving restaurant ecosystem had taken root. Key moments included Ruth Rogers's debut of her Italian eye-opener, the River Café, in 1987. Within a decade, Fergus Henderson, who gave the world the phrase "nose to tail eating," put his all-in philosophy on glorious display at St. JOHN, starting in 1994. Just after the turn of the century, in 2002, the Palestinian chef Sami Tamimi and the Israeli-born chef Yotam Assaf Ottolenghi opened a deli in Notting Hill, the first of more than a few places. As important as these openings were, most influential were all the chefs who opened their own places after passing through those kitchens (let us not forget Le Gavroche, which opened in 1967 and furthered the culinary ambitions of Marco Pierre White, Gordon Ramsay, Marcus Wareing, Pierre Koffmann, and countless other chefs of substance).

London is one of the greatest sprawling and living cities on the globe, and practically every cuisine in the world can be found there—from that of India, China, France, Spain, Japan, Indonesia, and everywhere in between. For the most part, things have only gotten better since Robuchon made his observation. Pre-Covid and pre-Brexit, everything needed for a vibrant restaurant scene was at hand. Fresh produce, pools of money, and industrious staff flowed in from the Continent and beyond. Menus burst with invention and excellence, and London diners responded with unbridled enthusiasm, queuing up earnestly in front of one new establishment after another, cheered on by a passionate food media. The pandemic has had a devastating effect on business all around the world and on the restaurant industry in particular. London has been no exception, with one not-so-minor footnote: The UK's departure from the European Union has complicated the matter. Still, London's restaurants continue to evolve and will thrive for years to come.

Note: It takes a special magic to run a successful restaurant. Under the best of circumstances that spell only lasts so long. Given the speed of change in the world lately, a few of these places may have closed between editing and publishing, but they will forever remain enchanting.

CONTENTS

A TASTE of LONDON

**The Restaurants and Pubs
Behind a Global Culinary Capital**

JOHN DONOHUE

Abrams Image | New York

For the past six years, starting in my home city of New York, I've made it my life's work to draw the world's restaurants. When I realized London's place as the potential culinary capital of the world, I was eager to go. I took two trips in the summer of 2018, and wow, did I have fun. I marveled at such unexpected sights as palm trees (who knew?) around town and an eye-popping number of Ferraris on the streets of Belgravia and Knightsbridge. I was blessed by impossibly clement weather. On my first trip, it didn't rain once in the whole three weeks, and though Londoners complained that it was far too hot, the low humidity and cool nights made it feel like a perfect autumn day for this New Yorker. I enjoyed great liberties as a single diner. On almost any night I could jump the queue at even the hottest spot and quickly be seated at the bar. And the long summer days meant I could eat at a decent hour and then continue drawing as late as nearly nine P.M.

To plan my London trips, I reached out to people who know and love the city, including chefs, restaurant owners, food writers, journalists who live there, and world travelers. Those who had been there before me guided me as I captured places new and old, expensive and affordable, high and low, and as much in between as was humanly possible. The restaurants in this book are organized by neighborhoods or groups of adjacent neighborhoods. London is gloriously large, and to an outsider it can seem like a swirling vortex of money, land, and history. The book starts with Covent Garden, and the chapters follow in a roughly clockwise fashion, first to the west and then back around to the east and then, as if being swept along by the whirlpool of wonder that is London, spinning out in the last chapter across the regions south of the Thames. There's an index and a neighborhood map in the back if you are looking for any specific places.

My process is simple. I work in ink on paper and from life, without corrections (later adding the color at home). My drawings take about twenty minutes, not counting the time it takes to find a place on the street where I won't be bumped into or otherwise disturbed. This proved essential in London, where I once dodged a daylight fistfight in Soho and another time had to endure the stare of a suspicious bobby while I was standing in the middle of the Strand. London's culinary and physical immensity suits me very well, for drawing brings me great peace, and if I could, I'd draw forever. I would never be tired of London! I'm grateful for my spare and loose style, which lets the viewer's mind seemingly fill in the details, perhaps from a memorable trip, or a recent visit. Either way, I hope my work enables everyone to picture London the way Samuel Johnson once saw it. "There is in London all that life can afford," he said. I couldn't agree more.

CHAPTER 1

COVENT GARDEN

Clos Maggiore

33 KING ST., WC2E 8JD

Known not only as the most romantic restaurant in London, but also as the most romantic in the whole world.

Homeslice Neal's Yard

13 NEAL'S YARD, WC2H 9DP

Pizza by the slice or a whole twenty inches.

The Ivy

1–5 WEST ST., WC2H 9NQ

I was very lucky growing up, surrounded by extremely loving and supportive women. My mum, Grandma (mum's mum), and Godmother Jocelyn (Grandma's best friend) encouraged all my passions, but none more so than my love of the art world. Drawing, sculpting, painting—you name it, I dabbled in it.

Stained-glass windows line the dining room.

Living in Central London meant it was easy for us to visit the latest exhibition opening, so I got all the inspiration needed for my next school project. My absolute favorite of these trips soon became our annual Christmas jolly: an exhibition followed by dinner at the Ivy, where chivalry and sweet treats haven't changed since its opening—there isn't a non-dairy ice cream or latest-fad pudding in sight—and Grandma and Jocelyn would always be greeted by the waiters like long-lost friends.

All of us had an insatiable sweet tooth, and the puddings at the Ivy were, and still are, what dreams really are made of. Flambé and Baked Alaska weren't things I'd experienced until my grandma ordered it here and, my gosh, what an unforgettable memory. Table side, flaming liquor being poured over the shiniest, softest-looking meringue mountain before it was cut in two while still flaming. It blew my mind and is still to this day the dish I will only ever eat at 1–5 West Street, London.

Now as I am a grown woman with a fine art degree and blossoming advertising career, our annual trip has evolved, and our roles have reversed; I now treat my mum, but it's always the Ivy and always the Baked Alaska at Christmas.

—*Francesca Meyrick-Cole*

J.Sheekey

28–32 ST MARTIN'S CT., WC2N 4AL

Fish pie and fashionistas.

Rules

34–35 MAIDEN LN., WC2E 7LB

Rules was intended to make a good impression on my suspicious parents. I had run away to London for graduate school and to live with my English boyfriend. I should have stayed in New York, like my parents and the rest of my family, forever. Like many native New Yorkers, my father isn't easy to impress. Standing over six feet tall and always bedecked in a suit and hat, he is an imposing figure. My father has been compared to Robert De Niro in *The Godfather Part II* on more than one occasion. The English boyfriend thought quintessentially English Rules would charm both of my parents—and, by extension, elicit a nod of approval.

Entering the dining room was like stepping into a piece of history, because, well, it is. Thankfully, there was so much to look at that the lack of cross-party conversation wasn't too awkward. And then the menu: *Game birds may contain lead shot.* This sounded like a challenge, and my father accepted it. As if still needing protection from the shooting party, his plate came with a wall of Yorkshire pudding surrounding the game. A diner at the next table actually stood up to gaze.

"Have some!" my father said and pulled off a chunk. "Thank you!" the fellow diner said, accepting. "I'm English, and I've never seen Yorkshire pudding like that." My father took a bite of his grouse—and got the promised accompaniment. Anyplace else, you might make a fuss if you found a bit of metal in your food. But not at Rules. "Incredible!" my father said.

When we spilled out onto Maiden Lane afterward, the street ebbed and flowed with the Saturday-night London throngs. "Hey! You talkin' to me?" a lad called out from a pack. "You talkin' to me?" Right actor, wrong film. My father stepped forward. "You talkin' to me?" my father replied. I inhaled. It had been going so well. The lad looked at my father, and my father took another step forward. "I like your hat," the lad said and returned to his mates. My father turned around, grabbed my English boyfriend around the shoulder, and started walking. "Great place," he said.

—L.B. Fisher

Game is the rule at Rules.

Trophy heads over the fireplace at Rules.

CHAPTER

2

SOHO

Wine and candles go hand in hand at the romantic Andrew Edmunds.

Andrew Edmunds

46 LEXINGTON ST., W1F 0LP

These days the restaurant has a gleaming, well-equipped, and highly professional kitchen on the ground floor of the building, adjacent to the dining room—exactly where you would expect it to be. But not so long ago, the kitchen was a tiny space at the back of the basement, and the prep kitchen was upstairs, in the building next door, occupying the back room on the top floor of 44 Lexington Street (the restaurant is at 46). I'm a theatrical agent, and my office is in the adjacent room. Every morning, the KPs would lug trays of meat, buckets of potatoes, and other ingredients up six flights of stairs. As the morning progressed and they started cooking, delicious smells would drift into my office. The KPs would carry the cooked food back downstairs, into the street, and into the restaurant next door. This went on for years, until Andrew decided to build the present kitchen.

—*Simon Sharkey*

BAO Soho

53 LEXINGTON ST., W1F 9AS

Forget the chicken and the egg. The real question is gua bao and queues. Which came first?

Bar Italia

22 FRITH ST., W1D 4RF

Open since 1949, it was long the only place apart from the Bagel Shop on Brick Lane serving until 4 in the morning. "We went there every night of the three years of my college days and for many years afterward," said one former Londoner who has been in the art business for decades. Bar Italia is such a sacred place for night owls that Pulp wrote a song about it during their 1990s heyday.

Barrafina

26–27 DEAN ST., W1D 3LL

Tapas with a difference—and a Michelin star.
A genuine Soho icon.

Bob Bob Ricard

1 UPPER JAMES ST., W1F 9DF

In the summer of 2018, my husband and I planned a special trip for our upcoming fifteenth anniversary. We considered returning to Maui, where we'd had a wonderful honeymoon, but one day, out of the blue, he asked if I might want to visit London. I'd only been there briefly in the late eighties, and the city would be completely new to him, so we decided to go. We're both fans of vintage—I may qualify as an actual nerd in that regard—so when searching for a restaurant that might serve the perfect special-occasion meal, I included words like "retro" and "elegant" in my Google searches.

Bob Bob Ricard kept popping up, and as I looked at pictures of the decor, I couldn't help but think that the place seemed straight out of the glory days of *The Grand Budapest Hotel*. Dining in a Wes Anderson movie sounded fabulous, and indeed it was. After a spectacular meal, we indulged in a BBR Signature Chocolate Glory, their spherical concoction that opens up when a warm sauce is poured over it. The filling was a delicious passion fruit gelée, so there was a bit of Maui on our anniversary trip after all.

—*Dyana Neal*

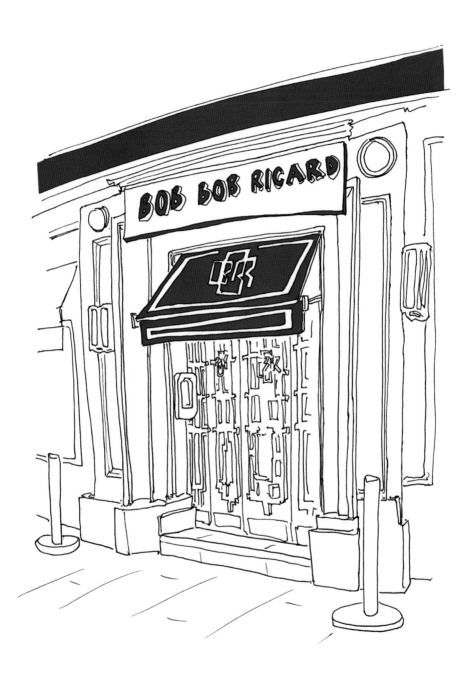

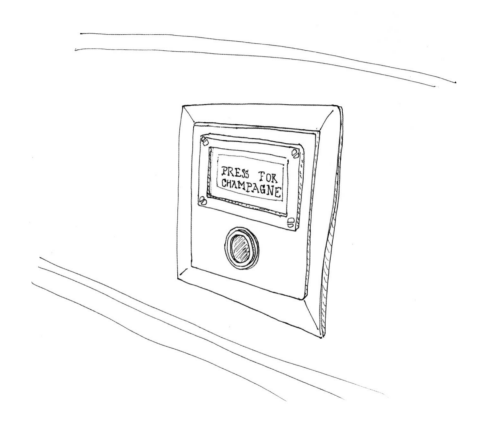

The famed tableside Champagne button.

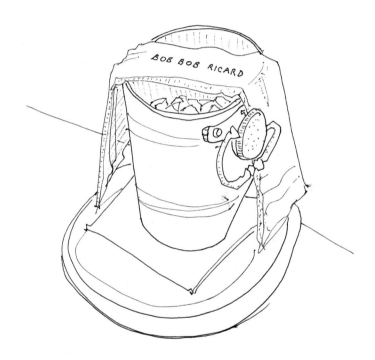

Champagne is always at the ready.

Bocca di Lupo

12 ARCHER ST., W1D 7BB

Maybe, just maybe, the best Italian restaurant
in Central London.

Brasserie Zédel

20 SHERWOOD ST., W1F 7ED

Soho's grand Parisian parlor that's cheap as
chips. Salade de carottes râpés, steak haché,
île flottante, et voilà!

The Gay Hussar

2 GREEK ST., W1D 4NB

The fabled place where politicians and political journalists once mingled over goulash has been reinvented by the folks behind Noble Rot (see page 182).

Golden Union

38 POLAND ST., W1F 7LY

Retro fish and chips in the center of London.

Hoppers

49 FRITH ST., W1D 4SG

It has queues like other places, but only
because its Sri Lankan hoppers, dosas,
sambals, chutneys, and karis are singular.

49 FRITH STREET

Jen Café

4–8 NEWPORT PL., WC2H 7JP

Seven steamed Beijing dumplings for five quid.

Kiln

58 BREWER ST., W1F 9TL

My mum loves eating out. Before her day off
work, every Wednesday, we choose a restaurant to go to. This is definitely easier said
than done. Finding new places is a challenge,
because she prefers to stick to the same spots.
Thai food is one of our favorite cuisines.
We always look forward to the food stalls at the
Thai New Year festival at a temple close to
where we live, but that event happens only once
a year. So, when I discovered Kiln, I immediately
had a special feeling in my stomach. Thai grill,
seafood, glass noodles baked in clay pots—
I showed my mum the menu right away.

When we went, we sat at the counter right in
front of the open fire. It felt like we were far
away from the London rain. I could tell she
was having fun. While we waited for the food,
we discussed the roles of the chefs, and she
pointed out our dishes being cooked. We were
so happy seeing our lamb skewers and grilled
chicken handed straight over from the fiery
kitchen. It was thrilling. My mum got impatient
while we were waiting for the clay pot and
waved at the waiter to ask when it would
arrive. Immediately after that, the chef placed
it right in front of us. My mum was so pleased.
When I find a new restaurant for us to try and
she enjoys it, it's the best feeling ever.

—Loletta Lee

Afropop is part of the rotation at Kiln.

Koya Bar

50 FRITH ST., W1D 4SQ

A special marriage of Japanese culinary traditions and brilliant British produce.

The little van that could.

Pizza Pilgrims

11 DEAN ST., W1D 3RP

I was in TV production. My brother was in advertising, and we were both a bit of a heady combination of being terrible at our jobs and hating them. It was 2011, and I was twenty-six and he was twenty-eight. We wanted to start a food business. We loved pizza but had no idea how to make it, so our whole idea was to buy a van and then use it to drive through Italy, finding the best pizza and finding the best food, and basically learning how to cook it all.

We bought the van in Sicily. It was a Piaggio Ape. Piaggo are the guys who make Vespas. "Vespa" is Italian for "wasp," and a Vespa is kind of for pleasure. An *ape* is a bee, and this is the working version of the same chassis. It was commissioned in 1948, straight after the war, as the vehicle that would help rebuild Italy. The idea was that it needed to be cheap, really easy to fix, very simple, and able to carry a lot of weight.

We drove from the southern tip of Italy up through Calabria, then to Campania, where I tasted Naples pizza for the first time and was like, "Oh my God, this is what it's all about." Then we spent a lot of time there learning about pizza. After that, up to Rome. Learned all about the Roman style of pizza and kept on moving up and then drove all the way back to London. But we hadn't quite established how slowly our van would go. We'd planned the trip based on Google Maps, which said ten days. Our Ape went only eighteen miles an hour, though, and it took us six weeks. Over the Alps, three miles an hour. It walked over the Alps, basically.

—James Elliot

Quo Vadis

26–29 DEAN ST., W1D 3LL

Once Marco Pierre White's patch, today it is the province of chef Jeremy Lee, who, among other culinary feats, might have created the city's best sandwich: one that encases smoked eel, creamed horseradish, and pickled red onion.

CHAPTER

3

MAYFAIR
AND
ST. JAMES'S

The Araki

Mayfair. £310 a head. Sushi as art. Food as luxury.

Bentley's Oyster Bar & Grill

11–15 SWALLOW ST., W1B 4DG

Chef Richard Corrigan's Mayfair temple to
pearlescent bivalves.

55

Connaught Hotel

CARLOS PL., W1K 2AL

Hélène Darroze and Jean-Georges Vongerichten, together inside one of the world's most famous hotels.

Gymkhana

42 ALBEMARLE ST., W1S 4JH

Muntjac biryani is the signature dish at London's premier Indian fine-dining restaurant. By 2022, Gymkhana was the in-crowd's choice.

Langan's Brasserie

STRATTON ST., W1J 8LB

A British institution reinvented, serving
celebrities and socialites since 1976.

Le Gavroche

43 UPPER BROOK ST., W1K 7QR

French old-school from the Roux dynasty. A category-defining restaurant since it first opened, in 1967, on Lower Sloane Street. The first English restaurant to be awarded a Michelin star and the first to ever be awarded three stars (it now has two).

Murano

20 QUEEN ST., W1J 5PP

At the back of the restaurant is our chef's table with a big window into the kitchen, and the space can be booked for private parties of up to twelve but also used for three smaller VIP tables. Whenever anybody proposes at Murano, it always happens at the little table in the corner. The staff keep a keen eye on what's happening and are ready for any eventuality. Two glasses of Champagne for a yes, or a scotch for a no.

A few years ago, one December, we had a chef's table of twelve, and they'd had quite a few drinks and were having a very good time, shall we say. We left them to it for about five minutes, and when we went back into the room, we discovered that they'd taken all the glassware and crockery off the table and put it in a corner. They'd taken out a tablecloth that had the printout of a ping-pong table and put that over the table. They'd set up a little net and, having brought racquets and balls with them, were playing table tennis on the chef's table. That's probably the most ingenious use of the space I've seen.

—*Laura Harris, Restaurant Director, Murano*

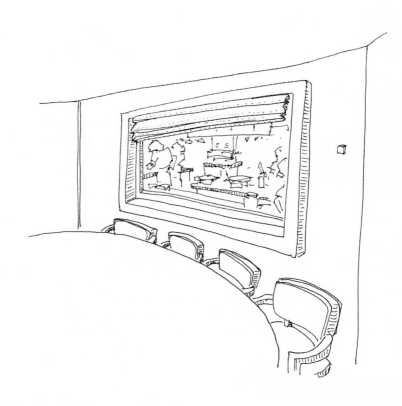

A window in the back room gives a view of the kitchen at Murano.

Pollen Street Social

8–10 POLLEN ST., W1S 1NQ

Chef Jason Atherton's flagship Mayfair tasting-menu restaurant.

Sabor

35–37 HEDDON ST., W1B 4BR

Barrafina alumni do a three-in-one Michelin-starred restaurant (The Counter and bar on the ground floor and the El Asador on the first floor) showcasing Spain's rich regional gastronomic diversity.

Scott's

20 MOUNT ST., W1K 2HE

Scott's is a London institution, but I first heard about it, funnily enough, after a paparazzo snapped Charles Saatchi fighting with his wife Nigella Lawson at the restaurant back in 2014. Shortly after, I visited the Mayfair eatery for the first time for dinner. I was sixteen and had already developed a hobby of trying new restaurants. Since then, I have come back to Scott's frequently because of its consistently excellent food, service, and reputation. It is a landmark in the London dining scene, which is a huge draw for me. Upon entering through the glass-fronted doors, I always feel a sense of arrival, of being somewhere important, when Donny, the long-serving doorman, greets me. I feel lucky to be there. The famed Art Deco–era window is off to one side, and the center of the room is filled with an iced display of daily catches and shellfish; it is no wonder most people decide to order what they can see rather than what's on the menu—they can observe how fresh it is. For me, I order the steak tartare for a starter and the grilled Dover sole as a main course. Maybe one day I will switch it up, but that day has yet to come. If both dishes come out perfectly each time, why change?

—*Alexander Khalaf*

69

Scott's circular window stands out in Mayfair.

Scully

4 ST. JAMES'S MARKET, SW1Y 4AH

After launching and running Ottolenghi's NOPI in 2011, Ramael Scully, who was born in Malaysia to a mother of Chinese Indian descent and an Irish Balinese father and who grew up in Sydney, opened his own place in 2018, where the flavors of his youth run wild.

Diners are greeted by a floor-to-ceiling open pantry, where the staff keep the salted egg yolks, pickled blueberries, preserved lemons and bergamots, and other wildly assorted homemade goodies.

Sketch

9 CONDUIT ST., W1S 2XG

London was on the first leg of my Euro trip with my cousin. I'd never been to Europe before, and I found out about Sketch through one of my college friends after she posted about it on Instagram. I was attracted to the pink, mid-century-modern vibes. Everything from the art to the soft pink chairs, I loved. I also had never experienced afternoon tea before, so I thought Sketch would be the perfect place for that first experience. However, since London was our first stop in Europe, we went ham and partied until six A.M.

By the time we got to Sketch later that day, I was half dying and half enjoying it. The most memorable thing was the music they played in the tearoom. It went from classical music to "Latch" by Disclosure, which was pretty great. Everywhere was a photo op, and I think I took a billion pictures of my cousin in every corner of the restaurant. The place is very "Instagrammable" to fit with today's social media craze, and we were no exception to that. Leaving Sketch, my cousin and I got asked by some older men if we were interested in doing exotic massages for $3,000. We think it was because we are Asian. We were very offended and sped off.

—Jasmine Tieu

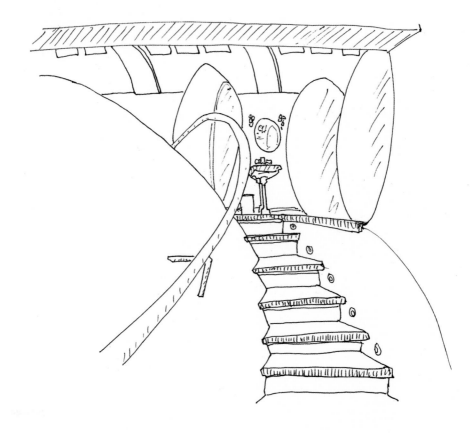

The sleek, futuristic bathroom pods at Sketch.

Veeraswamy

VICTORY HOUSE, 99–101 REGENT ST., W1B 4RS

London's original Indian fine-dining restaurant, established 1926.

Wiltons

55 JERMYN ST., SW1Y 6LX

One of the city's oldest restaurants, Wiltons, now on the gentleman's shopping street, began life as an oyster cart in 1742.

The Wolseley

160 PICCADILLY, W1J 9EB

Omelette Arnold Bennett here is the pick—one of the city's most regal breakfasts.

CHAPTER

4

WESTMINSTER, KNIGHTSBRIDGE, AND CHELSEA

A. Wong

70 WILTON RD., SW1V 1DE

If you're looking for Victoria's best restaurant, you might just happen upon London's best xiao long bao.

Claude Bosi at Bibendum

MICHELIN HOUSE, 81 FULHAM RD., SW3 6RD

Literally, the home of Michelin in London. Two stars, to boot.

Colbert

50–52 SLOANE SQUARE, SW1W 8AX

My now husband, Kip, and I traveled to London in 2017 on our first international trip together when we were dating. We always made it a point to try new restaurants so that we got a better understanding of the neighborhood/city/country where we were staying. One morning we happened upon Colbert and had the most wonderful breakfast (simple foods, exceptionally executed—porridge, caramelized grapefruit, and a perfect cappuccino). We returned there the next morning, marking our only duplicate restaurant visit on that trip. In the spring of 2022, we made another journey to London, this time to celebrate the end of my breast cancer treatment. Kip found a flat to rent for the week strategically located just around the corner from Colbert, so we could enjoy many more wonderful breakfasts there together.

—Meredith Wahlers

Dinner by Heston Blumenthal

66 KNIGHTSBRIDGE, SW1X 7LA

Meat fruit and molecular gastronomy sandwiched between Knightsbridge and Hyde Park.

Mr Chow

151 KNIGHTSBRIDGE, SW1X 7PA

Stylish Chinese food since the 1960s.

Regency Café

17-19 REGENCY ST., SW1P 4BY

The London greasy spoon: Art Deco, Formica tables, and bacon sandwiches.

CHAPTER

5

BAYSWATER, NOTTING HILL, HAMMERSMITH, AND KILBURN

Assaggi

39 CHEPSTOW PL., W2 4TS

Notting Hill's worst-kept Italian secret.

Casa Cruz

123A CLARENDON RD., W11 4JG

The perfect place in Notting Hill if you happen to be Prince Harry, Elton John, or Madonna. It's also where Rita Ora got caught breaking COVID-19 lockdown rules to celebrate her thirtieth birthday in 2020.

The Cow

89 WESTBOURNE PARK RD., W2 5QH

David Beckham and Ed Sheeran's favorite pub serves one of London's best pints of Guinness, but don't miss the oysters.

Farmacy

74 WESTBOURNE GROVE, W2 5SH

Vegan fun and cocktails.

Granger & Co.

175 WESTBOURNE GROVE, W11 2SB

Where people queue all morning for poached eggs and avocado on toast.

Khan's

13–15 WESTBOURNE GROVE, W2 4UA

Chicken tikka masala and lamb rogan josh on Westbourne Grove since 1977.

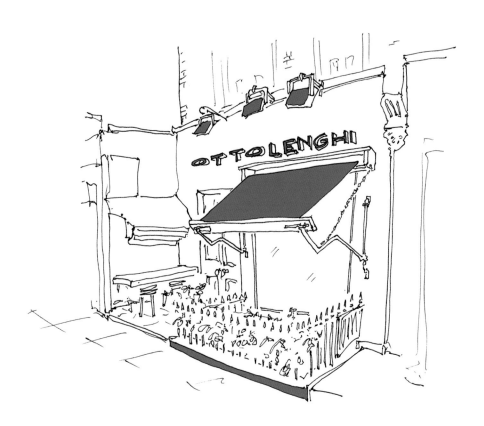

The sleek communal table that started it all.

Ottolenghi

63 LEDBURY RD. W11 2AD

My husband and I live in Notting Hill and are regular visitors of Ottolenghi on Ledbury Road. We do park runs on Saturday mornings and then like to treat ourselves to a special two-course breakfast of champions there— a sizzling shakshuka or brioche French toast with orange cream. We follow this with one of their pastries (a croissant for me, as they're full of flaky, buttery goodness!) along with a selection of their homemade spreads. What makes this place special is that you get to sit around that tiny shared table with others (usually locals if you're early). Inevitably everyone ends up swapping notes about Ottolenghi's books and his recipes. Our favorite is his chargrilled broccoli with chili and garlic. The first time we re-created that at home, it went down so well, people took doggy bags!

—*Deepika Misra*

Quartieri

300 KILBURN HIGH RD., NW6 2DB

Neapolitan pizza travels as far as Kilburn.

The River Café

THAMES WHARF, RAINVILLE RD., W6 9HA

I was doing a guest-chef week at the
Lanesborough Hotel about fifteen years ago.
With me were my sous chefs from the Red
Cat at the time, Laurence Edelman (who now
owns the Left Bank in New York City) and
Joey Campanaro (founder of the Little Owl,
also in NYC). We only had one full day off the
whole time, so we made a lunch reservation
at the River Café and laid plans for dinner at
J.Sheekey. We arrived at the River Café around
noon to sparkling wine and snacks, then pro-
ceeded to do three courses (with extra plates
from the kitchen) and three different wines to
match. I don't remember much but I do recall
an amazing slip sole with grapes and verjus
and a white Bandol from Château de Pibarnon.

Lots and lots of storytelling with espressos
and amaro followed. We did not realize the
whole place had cleared out or notice the staff
meal, but when we saw other patrons being
seated and food arriving, we decided to cancel
our reservation at J.Sheekey and stay at the
River Café. I've mostly blanked on the dinner,
but I do recall a woodcock dish with lardon,
laurel and chestnuts, and Conterno Fantino
Barolo. After dinner, more espresso and amaro;
we then poured ourselves into a car and went
back to the Lanesborough to drink old brandy.
They have a full room—a library—of it.

—*Jimmy Bradley*

The open kitchen at the River Café is
dominated by a big oven and a big clock.

The backyard at the River Café.

CHAPTER

6

KINGS CROSS, FITZROVIA, AND MARYLEBONE

Framed pictures cover every inch of every wall at Berners Tavern.

Berners Tavern

10 BERNERS ST., W1T 3NP

I took my favorite client to Berners Tavern in the first week it opened. You have to draw breath at the splendor of the room, the high ceiling, and the busy art gallery on every wall. We shared a leg of lamb and three bottles of claret, perched at a corner table with a view of the whole space. I'd had my eye on the cocktail list and implored my guest to try one for dessert. Two small chocolate-milk bottles with blue candy-striped straws appeared—and were emptied. Then a few more. A few "Cereal Killers" each later, we stumbled out into the night.

—Elliot Jacobs

Chiltern Firehouse

1 CHILTERN ST. W1U 7PA

Celebrities with a side of tricked-out comfort food.

Honey & Co.

25A WARREN ST., W1T 5LZ

For ten years, this was the location for some of London's best hummus at one of the city's sweetest restaurants. In 2022, the founders, chef couple Itamar Srulovich and Sarit Packer, relocated to Bloomsbury. Go find them at 54 Lamb's Conduit St.

Kitchen Table

70 CHARLOTTE ST., W1T 4QQ

I opened Kitchen Table in 2012 with my wife, Sandia, with an aim to serve modern British cuisine with creativity at its heart. Our daily-changing tasting menu is led by British produce and always takes inspiration from what is available with the seasons. For example, recently I was walking in the woods with my dog, Paxo, and spotted the rose hips just coming out. It reminded me that we had a rose hip paste at the restaurant that we hadn't used yet. When I was back in the kitchen, we made a dish of mussels glazed with rose hip. People's tastes change with the seasons, too; in the winter when it's game season we get deer and pheasant, which provides the perfect richness for cold weather, but in the summer months we'll use cooler, lighter ingredients like English peas, which are perfect at that time of the year.

The other aspect of our philosophy that is vital to Kitchen Table's identity is our dedication to transparency. This includes the sourcing of our ingredients locally, without any mysterious provenances—no strawberries in the middle of winter! We transfer this idea to our restaurant experience, with guests facing an open kitchen while they eat, watching each dish being prepared. I think it's really important to show the workings of the kitchen and create a dynamic between the chefs and the guests. It means that every night is different for us in the kitchen, too, not just because of the changing menu, but we'll have different guests and a different chemistry with them. Sometimes they'll engage with the chefs and ask a lot of questions, or sometimes we might have to turn up the music because nobody is talking. Last year, we refurbished the front space, which formerly had been our hot dog and Champagne bar, Bubbledogs, to create a lounge for guests. Guests start their meal there with snacks and aperitifs. While diners are sitting at the kitchen table for their main meal, we transform the lounge by changing the music and lighting so it's a place appropriate for petit fours, coffee and teas, and digestifs. Clearly, we like to keep everything in its place.

—*James Knappett*

Roti King

40 DORIC WAY, NW1 1LH

Cult-classic roti canai (Malaysian roti) and queues (an English custom) by Euston station.

CHAPTER

7

HIGHBURY, ISLINGTON, STOKE NEWINGTON, AND HOLLOWAY

The oven at Black Axe Mangal once wore a heavy-metal tattoo.

F.K.A.B.A.M. (Formerly Known as Black Axe Mangal)

156 CANONBURY RD., N1 2UP

Kate and I set BAM up in a very spontaneous manner. Our low budget hindered our fantasy restaurant, so we did what we could with what we had. The loud music, the dicks and pussies painted on the floor, and the dominatrix of a KISS oven are all totems that were put in place to detract attention away from me. I was terrified of opening BAM and used these elements as a shield to hide behind, like Jim Morrison singing with his back to the audience. I'm a little more confident nowadays, but these features have become key to the spirit of our tiny restaurant. We plan to paint the oven very shortly, but it's all a work in progress.

—Lee Tiernan, who opened Black Axe Mangal with his wife and business partner, Kate Mullinger Tiernan, in 2015

Primeur

116 PETHERTON RD., N5 2RT

We were never the kind of couple to make a big deal out of Valentine's Day. We're turned off by the clichés, the fixed-price menus loaded with heavy-handed puns, and the impossible-to-meet expectations. I don't remember why we chose to break our long-loved tradition of staying in, but on February 14, 2018, we ended up at Primeur. The little restaurant in Stoke Newington is easy to miss, only really detectable by the glow it casts on the outside pavement, but within that intimate space, over candlelight, we had the best meal of our lives. Ox heart, monk's beard, and a glass of red; our stomachs and hearts were filled that night. We returned for every special occasion after that. And my fiancé became a chef there, so now the enchanting little place that stole our hearts is an even bigger part of our lives.

—*Kayla Satzger*

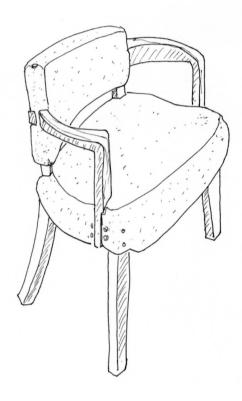

They say the chairs here are from the Savoy.

The space Primeur is in used to be an auto-repair shop before it became a restaurant.

Trullo

300-302 ST PAUL'S RD., N1 2LH

Quietly brilliant Italian. In many ways, underrated.

Westerns Laundry

Modern, British seafood, natural wines, and oh so much style. Dua Lipa–approved.

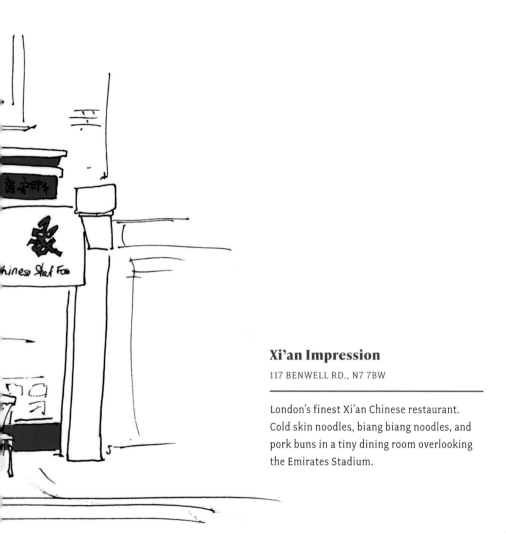

Xi'an Impression

117 BENWELL RD., N7 7BW

London's finest Xi'an Chinese restaurant.
Cold skin noodles, biang biang noodles, and
pork buns in a tiny dining room overlooking
the Emirates Stadium.

CHAPTER

8

DALSTON, HACKNEY, AND BEYOND

Brawn

49 COLUMBIA RD., E2 7RG

We have strong relationships with wine-makers/vignerons, and we normally host dinners and events whenever they are in town to allow our customers to share in their knowledge and experiences. A few years ago, there was a large fair in London of over one hundred winemakers from around the world. One evening we had about twenty of them at the restaurant. That volume of producers in one room and a cellar full of wine only meant one thing. It was a big party. By about four in the morning, the party was drawing to a close and the cleanup began.

We packed down, polished glasses, and set up for the next day. We turned the lights off, locked the door, and went home for a few hours' sleep. At six thirty A.M. I got a call from my alarm company saying the alarm had gone off. I hazily made my way to the restaurant to find the police already there trying to understand why there was a man in the restaurant running around with the doors locked. He spoke no English (he was from the deepest part of the Languedoc, in France) and the police were trying to calm him down. It turned out that he had fallen asleep in the toilet and woken up in complete darkness with no idea where he was. We eventually managed to get him to his hotel for some rest, and, needless to say, since then we always check the loos before we go.

—*Ed Wilson, who opened Brawn in 2010*

The evening crowd at Brawn.

Hill & Szrok

60 BROADWAY MARKET, E8 4QJ

We are on Broadway Market, at the end of London Fields, which, to be exact, used to be where cattle were kept before being taken to market in London. So, there's some of that heritage in our location. The shop is good because it gets younger people into a butcher's shop. We took away the notion of the counter and just have a big marble table that gives you a one-on-one experience with the butcher. When you walk into the shop, there's no barrier between you and the person serving you. We stand with our customers and go through what they need and cut what they want.

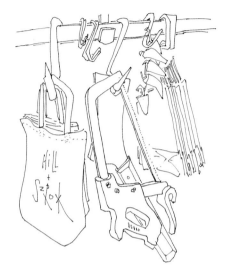

The furnishings at Hill & Szrok are not just for decoration.

We sell meat during the day and serve dinner at night. The cookshop part of the name came from the twelfth century, when we didn't have kitchens in the houses in London. Back then, you'd be able to go to a shop, buy stuff, and get it cooked there. It was sort of the first takeaway, but you'd be waiting around communal tables, and that's kind of where that whole idea came from.

We use different cuts of meat which we source from small local farms, so we try and visit them as much as we can. All our steak cuts are popular, obviously, but the one thing that people are most surprised and impressed by is the chicken. People are used to the supermarket, where the poultry comes cut up and in bags. They've never had a slow-growing bird. When you give someone something that tastes properly that's got loads of flavor and depth to it, people go, "Wow." As for me, I love a good pork chop. Every time I come here for dinner, even though it's cheap for me to eat here, I always have pork chops. This is the cheapest cut we do. I don't know, I just love it.

—*Luca Mathiszig-Lee, who opened Hill & Szrok in 2014*

The Laughing Heart

277 HACKNEY RD., E2 8NA

Happiness into the wee hours.

Mangal I

10 ARCOLA ST., DOWNS, E8 2DJ

Dalston, East London—home of the Turkish ocakbasi. No longer related to Mangal II.

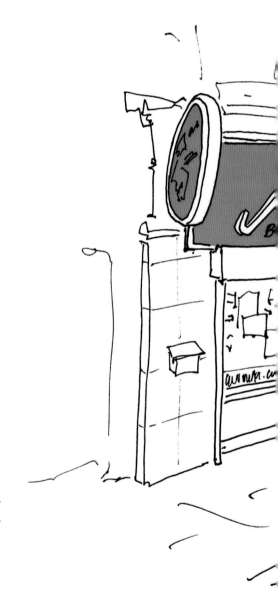

Mangal II

4 STOKE NEWINGTON RD., N16 8BH

Brothers Ferhat and Sertaç Dirik's spectacularly reimagined Turkish grill in Dalston, as appeared in 2018. It now has a blue façade.

The Marksman

254 HACKNEY RD., E2 7SJ

London's best pub food, perhaps.

P. Franco

107 LOWER CLAPTON RD., E5 0NP

Located as it is in the middle of nowhere, east of eastern London, you may not even notice P. Franco during the daytime, when its cold metallic shutters are closed, and the sign above it mentions the Great Wall of China in red. Only later in the afternoon, when you hear the shutters going up, does the real restaurant reveal itself. A place where you can have secret meetings or just catch up with an old friend, it's often full of international characters, backpackers, businessmen, fashion designers, or just people like me, a free spirit who loves food and nice wines. I am here with a concept developer for urban spaces, discussing food, wine, life, and love. The chef is cooking on the three burners at the back of the room, and the menu varies every week, depending on who is cooking. I chose crayfish, reminding me of summers at home in Stockholm, Sweden, and crayfish parties. The farmhouse cheese that we have is beyond loveliness. The bites are to share or just for yourself. They are splendid, beautiful flavors that explode in your mouth, especially when mixed with a nice glass of Meursault. Wow, the wines. They have a nice selection, of old ones and ones I have never tried. It's easy to drink one, two, three more glasses than you planned, just because you are in the kind of company that makes it feel right.

—*Katarina Cederholm*

There's one shared table and a lot of wine inside P. Franco.

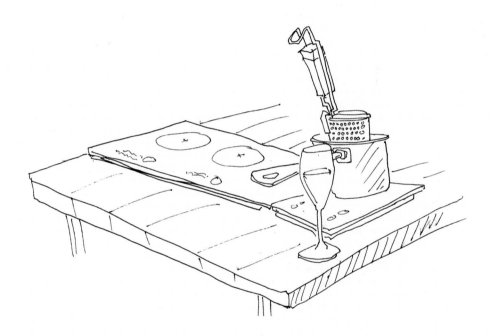

There isn't much more to the kitchen than these electric burners.

Yard Sale Pizza

Takeaway pizza for hipsters.

CHAPTER

9

HOXTON, SHOREDITCH, SPITALFIELDS, AND BETHNAL GREEN

Beigel Bake

159 BRICK LN., E1 6SB

Salt beef and smoked salmon twenty-four hours a day at the late-night beating heart of the East End.

BRAT

4 REDCHURCH ST., E1 6JL

Whole turbot, charcoal grill, an homage to the Basque Country. A beautiful thing all around, really.

The Clove Club

SHOREDITCH TOWN HALL, 380 OLD ST., EC1V 9LT

Supper club turned two-Michelin-starred dining room. Shoreditch's first, Shoreditch's finest.

E. Pellicci

332 BETHNAL GREEN RD., E2 0AG

Full English and a mug of tea. Iconic.

F. Cooke

9 BROADWAY MARKET, E8 4PH

Pie and mash, liquor, and jellied eels were served here for 120 years before it closed, in 2019.

Lyle's

Influenced by Noma, St. JOHN, and The Fat Duck, Lyle's is in lots of ways a crystallization of modern European dining in London in the present day.

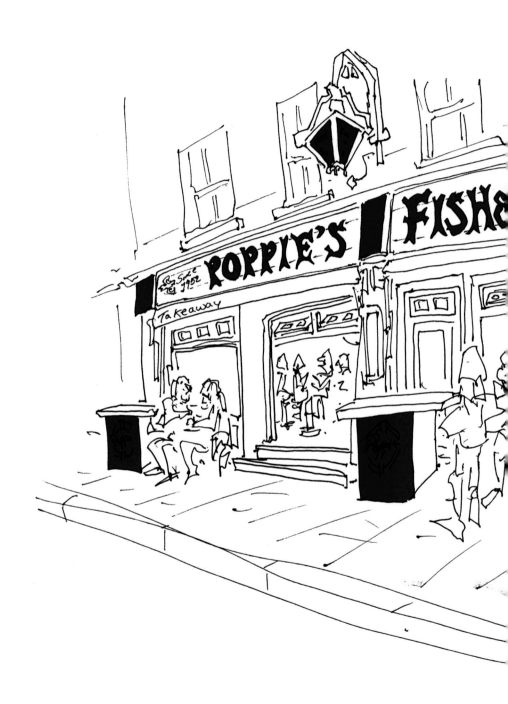

Poppie's Fish & Chips

6-8 HANBURY ST., E1 6QR

Salt, vinegar, mushy peas, and a gherkin, please.

Rochelle Canteen

16 PLAYGROUND GARDENS, E2 7FA

When I first knew that I was moving from
Malta to London nine years ago, I did the
most logical thing. I started compiling a list
of restaurants to visit. One of the restaurants
that made it onto the list from the very beginning was Rochelle Canteen. However, at that
time my mission was to try as many burger
and American BBQ restaurants as possible or
restaurants serving cuisines I couldn't easily
find back home. It was only after Anthony
Bourdain passed away and I re-watched all
the episodes of *Parts Unknown* that Rochelle
finally made it back to the top of my list.

In the London episode, Bourdain sat down
for lunch with Margot Henderson, the chef
and co-owner, and ate peas in their pod
and "vitello tonnato" and other simple yet
delicious things. It was then that I set about
making plans to go to Rochelle Canteen, but
I knew the visit had to be well planned. For
starters, it had to be on a sunny day—and
ideally a hangover-free one. Company was
also key; Rochelle requires the company of
good friends, the type who, apart from food,
enjoy a drink and wouldn't mind lazing in the
sun for a good few hours.

Food is served in a former bike shed surrounded by greenery.

Somehow that's exactly how the day turned out. It was one of those lazy afternoons that seem only possible on holiday in France or Italy. But no, this was bang in the middle of Shoreditch, in a sanctuary hidden away from the busy streets. We sat on the edge of the garden, started off with some Americanos (the alcoholic kind, not the coffee), and before we knew it, we had ordered all of the menu (or what was left of it). Skate in a buttery caper sauce and a Barnsley chop with green beans covered in a vinegary anchovy dressing were deemed to be the winning dishes. Nothing overcomplicated, just great ingredients, well executed.

It's the kind of place you don't want to tell anyone about because you want it to remain just as it is—a hidden gem that you take only your closest friends to and watch their surprise when you point out the door to the entrance and press the buzzer to be let in.

—*Gareth Agius*

Smoking Goat

64 SHOREDITCH HIGH ST., E1 6JJ

British-Thai late-night drinking food in a former Shoreditch strip club.

172

The Towpath Café

42 DE BEAUVOIR CRESCENT, N1 5SB

Cheese toasties, cortados, and spritzes by the Regent's Canal in De Beauvoir at East London's most cherished seasonal spot.

CHAPTER

10

HOLBORN, CLERKENWELL, AND FARRINGDON

The Eagle

159 FARRINGDON RD., EC1R 3AL

There were a lot of nice old pubs around
London being mismanaged by chain breweries,
and the Eagle was one of the first to be taken
over by a Londoner who cooked Marcella
Hazan—influenced Italianate food accompanied
by palatable wine. My favorite thing was a
robust fish soup and my favorite place to eat was
at the bar, where the young owner was smart
and amiable. It was a different time, before the
collapse of newspapers, when *The Guardian*
was next door on Farringdon Road, the Indy a
couple blocks over on City Road, and people still
drank at lunchtime (in front of their bosses).
The fringes of the city were rough back then—I
used to leave a dog biscuit by my Mini for an
urban fox I'd see trotting around southern
Islington mid-morning. But the Eagle was a
beacon. There was a lamp with a red shade
visible from the street. I loved the red lamp. It
made you want to go inside. The place had an
amiably bohemian feel and scruffily prosper-
ous clients and gave rise to a new generation
of chic-around-the-edge publicans.

—*Emily Green, who reviewed The Eagle in* The
Independent *shortly after it opened, in 1991*

177

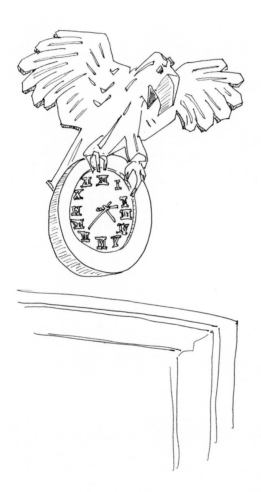

*An eagle watches diners at the place
where the gastropub was born.*

The Fryer's Delight

19 THEOBALDS RD., WC1X 8SL

Fish and chips the right way. Which is to say, fried in beef dripping.

Moro

34–36 EXMOUTH MARKET, EC1R 4QE

Twenty-six years young. Italian, North African, and Iberian-inspired timelessness by Sam and Sam Clark.

Noble Rot

51 LAMB'S CONDUIT ST., WC1N 3NB

London's most wide-ranging wine list. The food's quite nice, too.

The Quality Chop House

88-94 FARRINGDON RD., EC1R 3EA

Modern British cooking par excellence.

St. JOHN

26 ST JOHN ST., EC1M 4AY

It was a rainy afternoon in London when my boyfriend and I decided to get a late lunch at St. JOHN in Clerkenwell. St. JOHN is bright and airy, with high ceilings and twenty-foot-high skylights above the bar. Inside, the tables are sheathed in pristine squares of white paper, and the waiters don pressed white chef coats. Despite these formal features, St. JOHN has a relaxed atmosphere. The smell of fresh bread wafts through the air. My boyfriend was sitting across from me, slowly drinking his red wine. He ordered the kipper and potatoes, and I the pig's head with white beans. Over the course of our meal, as I spooned tender coins of pork fat into my mouth, I noticed that my boyfriend had become unusually quiet. Suddenly, his face reddened. He broke down and confessed that he didn't love me and probably never would.

Since the moment I'd laid eyes on him, I had been saving pictures of wedding dresses on my phone. Now, I just felt foolish. Tears were shed—I won't say whose. I'm certain that we were making the other diners uncomfortable. Regardless, the food was so good, I opted to prolong this tortured scene and order dessert. I sat there, arms half crossed, eating chocolate mousse while my now ex-boyfriend stumbled through a lengthy apology. By the time we left St. JOHN, the rain had cleared and the sun was out. I spent the rest of the day walking around London, heartbroken but so well nourished that I kept walking. I walked so long, my legs throbbed. I walked until the sun went down, and then I walked some more.

—*Liz Dosta*

The Bakery at St. JOHN is slightly more affordable.

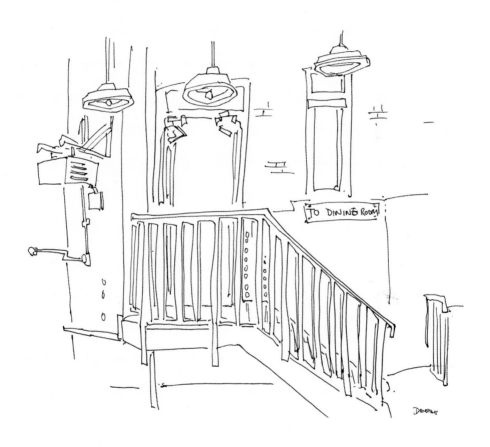

The inscription reads "TO DINING ROOM".

The proper temple of dining is up a few stairs.

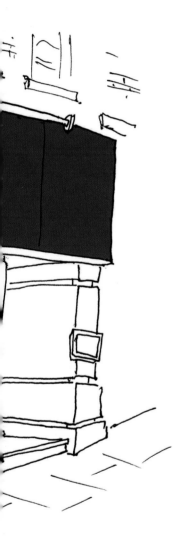

Vanilla Black

17–18 TOOK'S CT., EC4A 1LB

Very proper vegetarian fine dining. A casualty
of the pandemic, it closed in 2020.

CHAPTER

11

THE STRAND
AND
THE CITY

Duck and Waffle

110 BISHOPSGATE, EC2N 4AY

Fried duck and waffles forty floors above London's financial district, twenty-four hours a day.

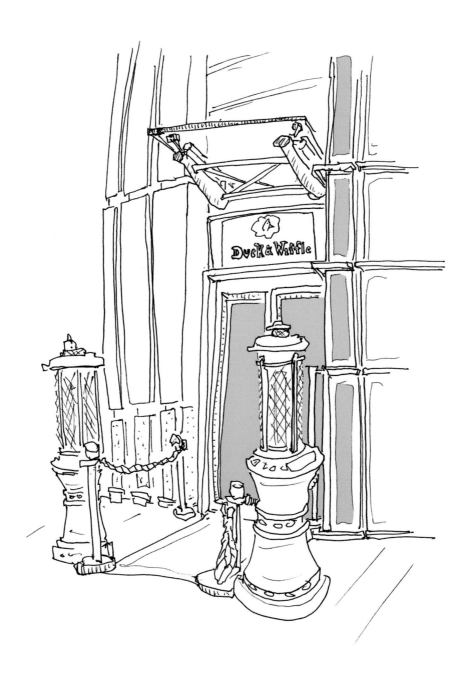

India Club Restaurant

143 STRAND, WC2R 1JA

India Club first opened in Craven Street in 1951, and its founding members included my parents, Dr. Dharm Sheel and Savitri Chowdhary, and several other UK residents, together with Krishna Menon, India's first High Commissioner in Britain, and some well-known people such as Lady Edwina Mountbatten, the wife of the last viceroy, and Prime Minister Nehru. Its guiding light was Menon, a leader of the India League, which was a powerful organization established in Britain to campaign for self-rule for India, and its central mandate was "to promote and further Indo-British friendship, that it should be non-political and that its membership should be on a broad basis."

To the many Indian students and professionals living and working in Britain, the Club offered a sanctuary with its homely atmosphere. It was somewhere you could take acquaintances to discuss issues of the day and forge friendships. When the Club moved to the Strand in 1964, the restaurant on the second floor offered authentic South Indian food. To this day, the restaurant, up a flight of stairs past the bar and lounge, has retained a 1960s café-like character akin to many eateries in India, which affords it a unique charm. You can still order a masala dosa, but the menu is no longer specifically based on South Indian recipes and now contains more mainstream Indian dishes.

My mother, who was drawn into the India League's campaign by Menon, was a regular at the India Club and remained so all her life. She was the author of *Indian Cooking*, one of the first Indian cookbooks published in Britain in 1954. As a connoisseur of Indian food, she frequently ate in the restaurant and sometimes made helpful suggestions to the chef.

In 2018, the Club was under threat of being redeveloped, and a huge campaign was mounted to save it. Because of its important historical connections with India and Britain, and the unique role it had played in providing a friendly cultural environment in the center of London, it was spared. Like my mother, I've been going there since it opened and am very glad it endures.

—*Shakun Banfield*

The Savoy

STRAND, WC2R 0EZ

My mother was visiting me in London, and our entire plan for the week revolved around finding the very best afternoon tea. As Americans who deep down felt there must be Brits somewhere in our ancestry, and who love their dry wit and their long history of writers capable of making the dampness of the region somehow so inviting, the concept of afternoon tea, for all ailments and celebrations, had always charmed us. My mother had read about the Savoy in various of her favorite mystery novels, and I knew of cucumber sandwiches from studying *The Importance of Being Earnest* in high school.

We entered in our best dresses. My mother, who typically consumes tea throughout the day either in her pajamas or at her desk at work in between students passing in assignments, was ready to have it the way it was intended: with sandwiches of every kind (no crust, of course). She usually drinks her tea out of a mug I made her in a ceramics class, a mug so large it resembles a soup bowl with a small handle attached. At the Savoy, the teacups were standard size, which gave her pause. The waitstaff were quick to refill them, though, and before long, we were starting to eye the restroom. We hurried, so as not to miss a moment of the next and most important course—the scones and the cakes. When the waiter heard us trying to surmise the source of clotted cream, he helped us with a smile. "It's the cream at the top of the butter," he said. In other words, the fat that is skimmed off the butter, which, if you ask me, is true decadence.

Drinking tea is nearly a religious experience for my mother, so it was nice to know that the Savoy is a true place of worship. The waitstaff reassured her they, too, brew the leaves for exactly four minutes—nothing less, nothing more. There is something to be said for enjoying tea this way, next to a piano player in an evening gown and below a chandelier that likely weighs as much as a car—to step out of your pajamas and into a dress that makes your walk a little grander. Instead of drinking tea out of to-go cups, you can feel decadent and delicate, full of complexity, and perhaps even as light on your feet as the accompanying Champagne, when sipping it at the Savoy.

—*Heidi Harrison*

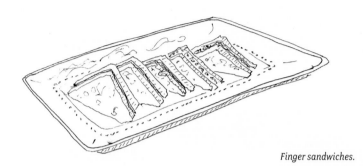

Finger sandwiches.

Teatime.

The tea trolley.

Simpson's in the Strand

100 STRAND, WC2R 0EW

Simpson's in the Strand, I've come to understand, is the second-oldest restaurant in London. I didn't know this before my visit there in 2019. To me, it was just a place that my dad would tell me stories about from his days working in the city. I must have walked past it a thousand times, but I had never looked inside. The full English breakfasts he would wax lyrical about (no doubt required to overcome the nights of excessive drinking City boys like him were known for in the late 1970s and early 1980s) held no appeal for me. I thought it was a relic of the past, and in some ways, it is, but in a brilliant way.

It turns out it's not just an upper-class greasy spoon but a true slice of history. It started as a chess café and became a favorite restaurant of Winston Churchill, who still has a table with his name on it.

My visit to Simpson's was booked for me by two close friends who knew I loved to cook and so thought I would enjoy the Sunday lunch carving course. It was so wonderful to tour the magnificent building and learn how to cook and carve a traditional roast.

I'm not sure that I can call myself a master carver (despite receiving a certificate), but slicing the most delicious ribs of beef I have ever eaten for my table of friends using a two-hundred-year-old silver carving trolley in the grand dining room of Simpson's in the Strand was an experience I will never forget. My dad was the first person I messaged after we left, and I wish it hadn't taken me thirty years to discover what he knew all along.

—*Nick Flynn*

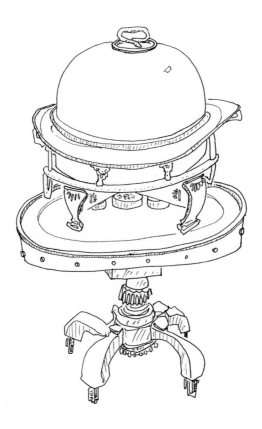

A two-hundred-year-old silver carving trolley at Simpson's.

Spring

SOMERSET HOUSE, WC2R 1LA

The finest vegetables and smartest uniforms tucked into the wings of a spectacular museum.

Sweetings

39 QUEEN VICTORIA ST., EC4N 4SF

One of the most amazing things about food as tradition is its ability to transport you. Not just across the earth (like when that new snack bar down the street from your apartment puts a papaya salad on the menu that takes you straight back to the alleys of Ho Chi Minh City), but also through time. Tradition, by definition, keeps change over time to a minimum. And when traditional foods are done right, they come as close as we can get to being the most immersive form of consumable virtual reality.

I find it fitting that I was introduced to Sweetings by a historian, my dining partner for a quick lunch before a flight out of London. When someone claims that the menu hasn't changed in over a hundred years, the natural skeptic in you might scoff; but when the heaping plates of unfussy seafood are actually served, sparse, direct, and mostly unadorned, it all clicks. The staff offer a hospitality that is polished but not overbearing. You get the sense that's because their ceremony of the business lunch has been performed so many times, it has become second (third, or fourth?) nature to them. Sweetings doesn't just feel like that old form of formal good-naturedness, it feels like the history of good-naturedness complied. With culture today moving faster than ever, it's quite refreshing to step through the heavy wooden doors of its royal blue façade and, at once, back in time. (Don't skimp on the puddings either . . .)

—David Zilber, food scientist, author, and former Director of Fermentation at Noma

204

The pre-service setup at Sweetings.

Lunchtime diners at Sweetings.

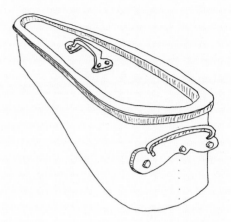

A fish poacher.

*Simple furniture goes with the
easy prices at Sweetings.*

SOUTH OF THE THAMES, FROM SOUTHWARK TO RICHMOND

Brunswick House

30 WANDSWORTH RD., SW8 2LG

Antiques, bric-a-brac, gin, cocktails—a unique
modern European brasserie in Vauxhall.

Chez Bruce

2 BELLEVUE RD., SW17 7EG

French class.

40 Maltby Street

40 MALTBY ST., SE1 3PA

A lot of people say that this arched, narrow spot is the best restaurant in London. This isn't hyperbole; they're probably right.

Franco Manca

3 & 3A MARKET ROW & 4 MARKET ROW, SW9 8LD

The original outpost of the Neapolitan
sourdough-pizza empire.

The Garden Café

GARDEN MUSEUM

5 LAMBETH PALACE RD., SE1 7LB

Only half a mile from Big Ben, across Westminster Bridge, on the south side of the river Thames, is Lambeth Palace, the historic home of the Archbishop of Canterbury, head of the Anglican Church. And adjoining this is St. Mary's, the former parish church of Lambeth (I claim a tenuous relationship here . . . a distant relative was vicar here in the mid-nineteenth century). A dwindling congregation saw the church close in the 1970s, but a new use was soon found for the building, which was transformed into the Garden Museum.

This would be a good enough attraction on its own, but in 2017 an award-winning restaurant was grafted onto the side of the museum, its expanses of plate glass and mellowing bronze shingles blending sympathetically with the ancient fabric of the church. But better still is the food. The head chef, George Ryle, is young and has a stunning pedigree. He buys ingredients daily, sourcing locally wherever possible.

His enthusiasm and imagination shine through the seasonal menu, which changes each day. The restaurant seems to specialize in unusual cuts of meat. Hogget saddle anyone? (To save you having to look it up, a hogget is a sheep older than a lamb but not quite mutton . . . so more flavor without being old and tough.) The first time I went there, damson ripple ice cream was offered as a pudding, and being the pudding person that I am, I was hooked at the outset.

While you're eating, you can gaze into the courtyard containing the grand tombs of the two father-and-son pioneer botanists—and successive head gardeners to King Charles I—John Tradescant the Elder and the Younger. And that of Admiral William Bligh RN, famous for having been cast adrift by a mutinous crew while sailing the South Seas. Where else in London can you dine in such esteemed company?

—*Jonathan Lingham*

There's a gravestone on the floor of the dining room at the Garden Café.

M. Manze

87 TOWER BRIDGE RD., SE1 4TW

Pie (eel) and mash since 1902. A Cockney classic.

Padella

6 SOUTHWARK ST., SE1 1TQ

I was on a business trip in London and found myself going back to Padella for four consecutive nights. It's true. I get weak in the knees when Italian food is even mentioned, but this place had something extra that made the experience addictive. Sitting at the bar (a must), I loved watching the tattooed chef and her team smiling, laughing, plating one dish after another, not at all concerned with the orders piling up on the screen. The kitchen was so small, it could only fit four cooks: One in charge of entrées, one of making fresh raw pasta, one juggling four pans above the flames, and the chef plating up. I had three dishes of pasta the first night. Sounds crazy, I know, but here is the thing: The dishes are just the right amount, light, and more than reasonably priced. With a view just over the chef, I simply looked at the dishes and asked the waiter for "that one." I hope to have the chance to revisit Padella soon and point at a couple of dishes again.

—*Avner Avidan*

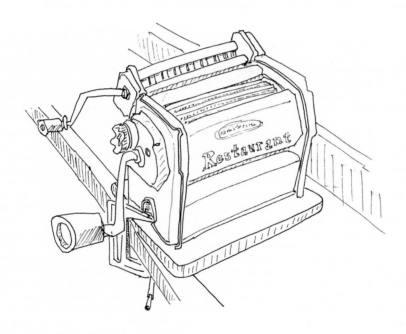

The pasta maker gets a good workout every day at Padella.

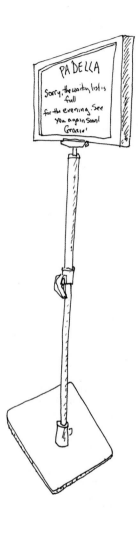

This is not what you want to see when you get here.

The queues have queues at Padella.

226

Petersham Nurseries

CHURCH LANE, OFF PETERSHAM RD., TW10 7AB

As a sometimes-suffering mother of two children in a school in Petersham, I had a "haven" to cheer myself up after attending occasionally frustrating meetings with teachers. Opposite a cow field at the end of a sandy road, it is one of those Arcadian places where you feel better the moment you enter through the gates. What initially presents itself as a nursery is actually much more. In addition to stunning plants, there's a restaurant for lunch or dinner under fern trees and bougainvillea.

Waitered seating is offered in the restaurant, but you can also simply select from the many freshly made items for sale in the shed and wander off with your tray to a table in one of the greenhouses. It is like a secret garden with a constant near-summer feel. Even on rainy days it retains its magic.

—*Elisabeth v. Kospoth*

Elephants guard the entrance to the dining room.

Pinocchio sits sentinel over the dining room.

Restaurant Story

199 TOOLEY ST., SE1 2JX

In the beginning, I had this idea that diners would bring a book, and they would leave part of their story with our story, and it would be kind of an exchange. The success of this was phenomenal. The majority would write inside the book, why they left it, what it meant to leave it behind—whether it was a childhood favorite, a gift, or something along those lines. So many diners came and left a book that I didn't have anywhere to put them all. We started to give a percentage of the books to charity, to schools, to libraries, though we kept some special books from close friends and family and regular diners. We evolved and grew, and we recently refurbished the room. The Connor Brothers did the art. I told them my vision with the refurbishment, and they felt that Pinocchio was a good fit. "Never let the truth get in the way of a good story" is something that I'll say flippantly at times. And one of the Connor Brothers' pieces in the hall has a favorite quote of mine: "The power of a story grows with every retelling."

—Tom Sellers, who founded Restaurant Story in 2013

Oblix (the highest grill in town), Aqua Shard (where it's all about the view), and Hutong (northern Chinese and some of the city's finest duck) are found on floors 31–33 of Europe's tallest building.

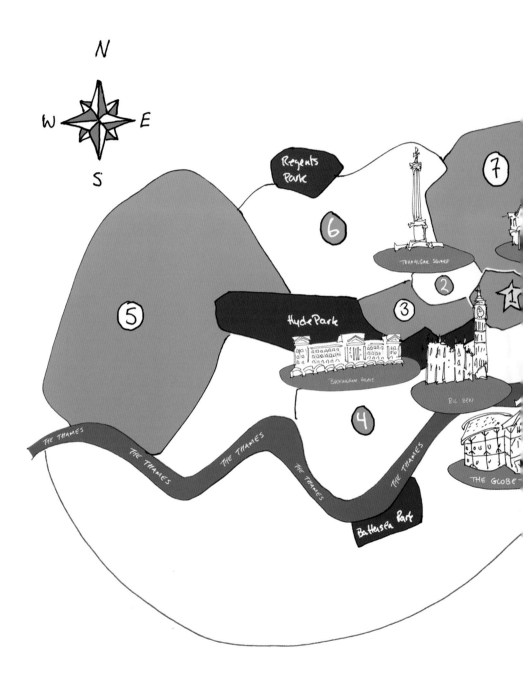

N
W E
S

Regents Park

6

7

TRAFALGAR SQUARE

5

2

3

HydePark

1

BUCKINGHAM PALACE

BIG BEN

4

THE THAMES

THE THAMES

THE THAMES

THE THAMES

THE THAMES

THE THAMES

Battersea Park

THE GLOBE

London Map Key

1   Covent Garden

2   Soho

3   Mayfair and St. James's

4   Westminster, Knightsbridge, and Chelsea

5   Bayswater, Notting Hill, Hammersmith, and Kilburn

6   Kings Cross, Fitzrovia, and Marylebone

7   Highbury, Islington, Stoke Newington, and Holloway

8   Dalston, Hackney, and Beyond

9   Hoxton, Shoreditch, Spitalfields, and Bethnal Green

10 Holborn, Clerkenwell, and Farringdon

11 The Strand and the City

12 South of the Thames, from Southwark to Richmond

ACKNOWLEDGMENTS

As with *All the Restaurants in New York* and *A Table in Paris*, this
London collection is far from an individual accomplishment. So many
talented and wonderful people helped make this happen, and I want
to thank them from the bottom of my heart. Drawing is my life's work,
and I couldn't do it without their assistance.

First, I owe my dedication and determination to put pen to paper
to my wife and children. Without them I wouldn't have started, or
be where I am. My editors, Holly Dolce and Soyolmaa Lkhagvadorj,
saw more possibility in my work than I could have imagined. Meg
Thompson and Cindy Uh as well. And I was only able to complete
this book through the extraordinary understanding of Brooklyn
Community Services' leadership (current and former), including
Janelle Farris, Marla Simpson, Sonya Shields, and Kristina Reintamm.

My wife, Sarah, worked grade-A wizardry with her extended family
and friends abroad to provide me with housing. Thank you, Elisabeth
v. Kospoth and Rhoda Eitel-Porter, for providing me with such hospitality and comfort. Harald and Ulrike von Waitz, you are the best!

The following folks were instrumental in their own way in the success
of the book and the happiness of my London trips: Zoë Blackler, Jimmy
Bradley, Corey Chow, Adam Coghlan, Aileen Corkery, Rosie Dastgir
and John Gapper, Jake Elliot, Blake Eskin, Dorothy Fields, Lara Fisher,

Sylvie Freedman, Catherine Harris, Diana Henry, Michael Hurwitz, Rose Kernochan, Lisa Linder, Sandy Markwick, Brenda Marsh, Alex McBride, Emily Nunn, Mark Rozzo, Anthony Schneider, Tricia Vuong, and Guy Wiggins. Zoë Pagnamenta deserves special note in this department.

A special thanks goes out to everyone whose name appears in this book with a story or a set of suggestions.

The considered and wise counsel of Paul Halligan, Erik Gardner, Mike Gracia, John Wyka, William Stenhouse, and Dušan Sekulovic has been invaluable. Betsy Andrews, Katie Baldwin, Sohrab Habibion, Doug Hamilton, Randall Eng, Paul Greenberg, Cressida Leyshon, Milda De Voe, and Sean Wilsey all played their part. My late parents and my brothers and sisters, too, as well as my beloved father-in-law. Additionally, Patty Diez and Amanda Kludt provided early and continued support.

Thank you, too, to the team at ABRAMS, including Jenice Kim, Margaret Moore, the publicity and marketing teams, Glenn Ramirez, and Kathleen Gaffney. Thank you, Michael Carusillo, for all your assistance. The amazing folks at Skink Ink, especially Philip, Vera, Brandon, Casey, Ben, Kylie, Zoe, and everyone else there, really made this project possible. And above all, to everyone who has shared a story, visited my website, or ever ordered a print—thank you.

INDEX